AF266280

Our Connected World

An In-depth Examination of Globalization

by Thomas T. Taylor

Copyright 2023 Archieboy Holdings, LLC.
All rights reserved.

Formatted, Converted, and Distributed by eBookIt.com
http://www.eBookIt.com

ISBN-13: 9781456641405(paperback)
ISBN-13: 9781456641290 (ebook)
ISBN-13: 9781456641412 (audiobook)

No part of this book may be reproduced in any form or by any electronic or mechanical means including information storage and retrieval systems, without permission in writing from the author. The only exception is by a reviewer, who may quote short excerpts in a review.

Although the author and publisher have made every effort to ensure that the information in this book was correct at press time, the author and publisher do not assume and hereby disclaim any liability to any party for any loss, damage, or disruption caused by errors or omissions, whether such errors or omissions result from negligence, accident, or any other cause.

This publication is designed to provide accurate and authoritative information with regard to the subject matter covered. It is sold with the understanding that the publisher is not engaged in rendering professional services. If legal advice or other expert assistance is required, the services of a competent professional should be sought.

The fact that an organization or website is referred to in this work as a citation and/or a potential source of further information does not mean that the author or the publisher endorses the information the organization or website may provide or recommendations it may make.

Please remember that Internet websites listed in this work may have changed or disappeared between when this work was written and when it is read.

Dear Esteemed Reader,

Thank you immensely for choosing this book to join your collection. We imagine that you've already embarked on an exploration of ideas within these pages, and we couldn't be happier about it!

Now, if you find yourself chuckling, pondering, or even debating with the words in front of you, we'd absolutely love to hear about it. If you can spare a few moments to pen down your thoughts in a review, we would be as delighted as a dictionary on a spelling bee!

An Amazon review would be excellent - but hey, we're far from picky. Whether it's a scribble on the back of a grocery list, a tweet, or even a message in a bottle (though that might take a while to reach us), your feedback is gold.

Writing a review might not be as fun as a spontaneous dance-off, but we promise it'll bring grins to our faces, warmth to our hearts, and incredibly valuable insights to future readers.

With Gratitude,

Bo Bennett, PhD
Publisher
Archieboy Holdings, LLC.

Table of Contents

Introduction

In our quest to understand the complex web of relationships and interactions that make up our world today, we find ourselves at the doorstep of an intriguing phenomenon - globalization. It's a word we've all heard, a topic of dinner table debates, political dialogues, and academic discourses. Yet, do we truly grasp its expanse? The forthcoming chapters of "Our Connected World: An In-depth Examination of Globalization" seek to decode this phenomenon, illuminating the pivotal moments of its historical journey, the forces driving it, and the sweeping impacts it has on our global economy, politics, environment, and society. This exploration will take us from the familiar landscapes of North America to the emerging markets of Asia and Africa, the hallowed institutions that guide its path, and the digital frontiers of the 21st Century. Critiques will not be shied away from, as we assess the future of globalization in light of economic, social, cultural, and environmental concerns. So, let's begin, shall we? Onwards to a journey of discovery, analysis, and understanding.

Definition of Globalization

Just as a sculptor begins with a vague block of marble and carefully chisels away to reveal the masterpiece within, we must first shape the amorphous concept of globalization into a discernible form. It is not a single entity, but a compound of various aspects, interwoven and interconnected. Globalization, at its most basic, refers to the increased interdependence and integration of countries economically, socially, culturally, and politically. It represents the transnational circulation of ideas, languages, popular culture, and human beings.

Yet, the term 'globalization' itself is not as old as the concept it encapsulates. Historians and economists will argue that the seeds of globalization were sown centuries ago, with trade routes connecting the far corners of the ancient world. Yet, the term 'globalization' first came into widespread use in the 1980s, reflecting a world increasingly interconnected by new technology, international trade, and the flow of information, capital, and people.

Now, this definition may appear simple on the surface, but let's dig a little deeper. At the heart of globalization is the concept of 'connectedness.' This is not merely a physical connection, like that of trade routes, nor a virtual connection, such as the internet, but rather a complex system of interwoven relationships that transcend borders and create a global network of exchanges and interactions.

This connectedness is multidimensional, encompassing economic, political, social, and cultural aspects. Economically, globalization refers to the global distribution of the production of goods and services, facilitated by an open, free, international trade system. Politically, it can be seen in the rise of supranational bodies, like the United Nations, the World Trade Organization, and the International Monetary Fund. Socially and culturally, globalization refers to the transnational dissemination of ideas, languages, or popular culture through acculturation.

On another layer, the scale of globalization can vary. It can be vast and global, impacting the whole world, or it can be more regional, affecting a limited number of nations within a particular geographic area. It can also be bilateral, involving just two countries.

However, while the process of globalization seeks to make the world more interconnected, it does not mean it makes it homogeneous. One of the most fascinating aspects of globalization is how local cultures adapt and respond to global influences. The results are not uniform, leading to a paradoxical phenomenon of 'glocalization' - the adaptation of global ideas into local contexts.

Finally, let's keep in mind that globalization is not a one-way process. It is a continuous, dynamic, and reciprocal process. Countries, societies, and cultures influence each other and evolve together. However, the impacts of globalization are not evenly distributed and have led to significant disparities which we will explore in subsequent sections.

To summarize, globalization is an intricate, multifaceted process that fosters interdependence and integration among nations, economically, politically, socially, and culturally. It is the shaping force behind the interplay of global unity and local diversity, creating a world that is interconnected, but not homogeneous. This understanding provides us with a basis to delve deeper into the historical development of globalization and the diverse dimensions it influences.

Historical Overview of Globalization

To understand the essence of globalization, we must navigate the corridors of time and chart its journey through history. Although the term 'globalization' gained prominence in the late 20th century, its roots extend much deeper into the annals of time. Tracing its footsteps, we can begin to comprehend how historical events have shaped the complex and multidimensional entity it is today.

Dipping our toes in the early pool of human civilization, the concept of globalization might seem anachronistic. Yet, even then, humans began to reach beyond their immediate surroundings, prompted by curiosity, survival, or ambition.

Trade routes like the Silk Road and the Incense Route were more than just pathways for goods; they were the sinew connecting distinct cultures and societies. These ancient arteries of commerce allowed not just the exchange of tangible goods, but also intangible elements like ideas, beliefs, and technologies.

The Age of Discovery in the 15th and 16th centuries propelled globalization onto a new trajectory. Voyages of explorers such as Christopher Columbus and Vasco da Gama helped stitch the world together by sea, transforming the world from a series of "islands" into an interconnected web of trade and exchange. This period brought an unprecedented level of interaction between the East and West, fomenting a process of cultural exchange and economic integration.

With the advent of the Industrial Revolution in the late 18th and early 19th centuries, the pace of globalization rapidly accelerated. Innovations in transportation – steamships, railways, and later, aviation – drastically reduced the 'friction of distance.' Meanwhile, telegraph and telephone communications made it possible to share information across continents in a matter of minutes. It was during this period that we began to see the emergence of global financial markets, multinational corporations, and international institutions.

The 20th century, however, marked a critical turning point in the narrative of globalization. After the cataclysmic World Wars and the Great Depression, countries sought to create a more stable international system. The establishment of the United Nations, the World Bank, and the International Monetary Fund was an embodiment of this aspiration. Moreover, the rapid technological advancements, especially in information and communication technologies, knitted the world closer together, shrinking the temporal and spatial gaps that had once separated societies and cultures.

Yet, it's important to note that this journey of globalization has not been a smooth sail. The currents of history carried with them waves of opposition and backlash. Globalization has been - and continues to be - punctuated by periods of contraction or 'deglobalization,' often resulting from conflicts, economic downturns, or resistance to foreign influence.

Today, we stand at a juncture where globalization is under scrutiny, magnified by the 21st century's unique challenges, such as digital disparities, pandemics, and climate change. As we venture further into the 21st century, we must grapple with these complexities, balancing the need for global cooperation with respect for local diversity and autonomy.

In this vein, the following chapters will explore the history of globalization in greater detail, examine the forces that drive it, assess its multifaceted impacts, and ponder its future. This brief journey through the timeline of globalization sets the stage for the rich tapestry of perspectives and experiences that define our connected world.

Chapter 1: In-Depth History of Globalization

As we delve deeper into our exploration of globalization, it's time to turn our lens to the past. Think of this chapter as a time machine, transporting us across epochs and eras. We will journey from the ancient and medieval periods, when rudimentary trade networks spanned continents, through the Age of Discovery that brought about a seismic shift in the world order. We'll witness the monumental changes wrought by the Industrial Revolution and track the rapid advances of the 20th century. Throughout this historical sojourn, we'll uncover compelling case studies, examining the benefits and problems they brought to bear on societies worldwide. This, in essence, is a tour of the grand tapestry of history, providing us with a profound understanding of how our interconnected world came to be.

Ancient and Medieval Periods

When we consider globalization, it's easy to regard it as a phenomenon of the modern world, brought on by recent technological and economic developments. But, in fact, its roots run deep into our shared history, reaching back to ancient and medieval periods.

In the ancient world, the precursors to globalization were already in place. Think of the Silk Road, an epic network of trade routes stretching over 4,000 miles from China through Central Asia to the Middle East and on to Europe. Silk, spices, and precious metals flowed in one direction, while technology, ideas, and religion moved in the other, knitting together vastly different cultures in a web of exchange and mutual influence.

Or consider the Phoenicians, a civilization that occupied what is now Lebanon around 1200 BCE. Their skill at sea trade and their development of a phonetic alphabet that influenced Greek and Latin script, formed the basis for the communication revolution to come.

The Roman Empire, from 27 BCE to 476 CE, also played a critical role in the nascent globalization of the ancient world. Its comprehensive road and sea systems, coupled with a common language and legal framework, facilitated the free movement of goods, people, and ideas across a vast territory.

Transitioning to the medieval period, we witness the sprouting seeds of globalization in various forms. The rise of Islam in the 7th century, for instance, created a vast empire where goods, knowledge, and faith circulated. Notably, Islamic scholars preserved and built upon the ancient knowledge of Greeks and Romans, passing it on to Europe during the Renaissance.

Between the 11th and 15th centuries, the age of exploration sprouted. It was an age when traders like Marco Polo voyaged to the East, introducing Europe to Asian commodities like silk, spices, and porcelain, stoking demand and setting the stage for the later Age of Discovery.

During these periods, we see a world becoming gradually more interconnected, with societies influencing each other through trade, cultural exchange, conquest, and religion. Globalization, as we understand it today, did not emerge ex nihilo; it was built on a foundation of historical interactions, shaped by the grand narrative of human civilization. Remembering this not only provides valuable context but also imbues our understanding of modern globalization with the depth and nuance it deserves.

Globalization in the Age of Discovery

If the ancient and medieval periods planted the seeds of globalization, the Age of Discovery, roughly spanning the 15th to 17th centuries, watered those seeds into verdant growth. This era marked by exploration and expansion, catalyzed by advances in navigational technology and a rising appetite for global trade, brought an unprecedented level of interconnectivity to the world.

Anchoring the Age of Discovery were iconic figures like Christopher Columbus and Vasco da Gama. Columbus, under the patronage of the Spanish monarchy, famously sailed west in 1492, inadvertently connecting the Old World of Europe, Asia, and Africa with the New World of the Americas. A few years later, Vasco da Gama charted a sea route from Europe to India, bypassing the Silk Road and heralding a sea change in global trade routes.

These explorations unlocked a new chapter of globalization, characterized by the creation of permanent links between continents, the establishment of new trade networks, and a subsequent wave of cultural, biological, and economic exchanges now known as the Columbian Exchange. Goods, ideas, plants, animals, diseases—everything became part of the global exchange. It was a time of great opportunity, and also, a time of great upheaval.

Yet, we should not overlook the darker sides of this Age of Discovery. The search for new routes and resources led to the colonization and exploitation of native populations in the

Americas, Africa, and Asia. Millions were subjected to the transatlantic slave trade, the brutal corollary to these expansive trade networks. This aspect of globalization—the ruthless pursuit of wealth and power, often at the expense of human rights and equality—remains a sobering legacy of this era.

Furthermore, the homogenization of cultures and loss of indigenous knowledge were, and continue to be, poignant consequences of global integration. The spread of European languages, religions, and cultural practices often occurred at the expense of local traditions and ways of life, a trend with lasting implications that still echo in our current globalized world.

The Age of Discovery set the stage for the next major leap in globalization, the Industrial Revolution. But it left an indelible mark on the world, establishing a global network of economic and cultural exchange that was unprecedented in scale and speed. As we journey through the history of globalization, we carry with us the legacies of this era, both inspiring and cautionary, shaping the path that lies ahead.

The Industrial Revolution and Globalization

The Industrial Revolution, starting in the late 18th century, can be seen as a momentous accelerator of globalization. It was a period characterized by rapid technological advancements, mass production, urbanization, and profound socio-economic transformation. The world saw a shift from agrarian, rural societies to industrial, urban ones, with machines, factories, railways, and later, the telegraph, becoming the new normal. It was as if the world had suddenly stepped on the gas pedal, and there was no going back.

First ignited in Britain, the revolution's sparks caught on in Europe, North America, and eventually the globe. The invention of the steam engine, power loom, spinning jenny, and the cotton gin—these were not just technological breakthroughs but global game-changers. They increased productivity exponentially, but they also made the world smaller. For the first time in history, goods could be produced on a massive scale and transported over long distances quickly and economically.

The advent of railways and steamships transformed the landscape of trade and communication. These advances opened up remote areas to commerce, integrated national markets, and forged closer economic interdependence among nations. You could now sip tea from India in your parlor in England, or don the latest European fashions in the streets of New York—globalization had a new and potent vector.

At the same time, a new class of industrial capitalists emerged, who, with their newfound wealth, began to influence state policies. Protectionist barriers were gradually dismantled, and free trade became the driving economic ideology, further fueling globalization.

Yet, not unlike the Age of Discovery, the Industrial Revolution also had a shadow side. With urbanization came unhealthy living conditions in crowded cities. The gap between the rich and the poor widened as factory owners amassed wealth on the backs of cheap labor. On a global scale, the Industrial Revolution deepened economic and power imbalances. Industrialized countries, mostly in Europe and North America, grew in wealth and influence, often at the expense of their colonies or less developed nations which supplied raw materials but had little share in the resultant wealth.

It's critical to underscore that the ecological footprints of this era are still visible today. The unprecedented scale of industrial production and use of fossil fuels initiated an era of massive environmental transformation, a prelude to our current climate crisis.

The Industrial Revolution, by its conclusion, had irrevocably changed the face of the world. It gave globalization its second significant push, and in its wake, set the stage for the 20th century—a time that would see globalization take flight in ways unimaginable. But the narrative of the Industrial Revolution also serves as a stark reminder that progress and power, if unchecked, can leave deep scars—both on humanity and the planet.

Globalization in the 20th Century

As we stride into the 20th century, the pace of globalization quickens. While globalization as a concept had been blossoming for centuries prior, it was in the 20th century that the world truly became a global village, shaped by world wars, geopolitical realignments, technological advancements, economic liberalization, and a profound shift in cultural perceptions.

The two world wars, while tremendously destructive, inadvertently accelerated globalization. The wars necessitated mass mobilization of resources, cross-border alliances, and collective defense mechanisms. Out of the ruins of World War II, we witnessed the birth of global institutions like the United Nations, the World Bank, and the International Monetary Fund. These institutions were founded on the belief that international cooperation and economic integration were the best ways to prevent future conflicts.

This belief also fueled the push for economic liberalization post World War II. With the Bretton Woods agreement, a system of monetary order was established. Trade barriers were dismantled, currencies were made convertible, capital became increasingly mobile, and the world market began to integrate like never before.

Parallel to these geopolitical and economic shifts, the 20th century also heralded a technology revolution. From air travel to television, from computers to the internet, these inventions shrank distances and redefined the concept of time and space. You could fly from London to New York in hours, watch the moon landing from your living room, and communicate with someone halfway across the globe in an instant. With the advent of the internet towards the end of the century, information began to flow freely, transcending national borders, ushering us into a new digital era of globalization.

Let's not forget the social and cultural dimensions. Mass media, tourism, and immigration all played their part in making cultures more intermingled than ever. We saw the rise of global celebrities, Western culture influencing the East, Eastern culture influencing the West, and all manner of fusion in between.

Yet, despite these advances, the 20th century was not without its growing pains. The benefits of globalization were not equally distributed. Economic liberalization led to growth, but also created disparities. As capital and corporations crossed borders, so did economic crises. The digital divide added a new dimension to global inequality. Cultures came into contact, but also into conflict. The very technologies that brought us together also had environmental costs, a bill that future generations would have to foot.

However, in the grand scheme of things, the 20th century was undoubtedly a defining moment in the story of globalization. It marked a shift from a world of separate nations to a truly interconnected global community. It set the stage for the next wave of globalization in the 21st century—a wave marked by digital technology, increased interdependence, and fresh challenges. A wave we are riding today. As we stand on the shoulders of the 20th century, we should appreciate the view but also be mindful of the pitfalls, for the journey of globalization is far from complete.

Case Studies and Their Outcomes (Benefits and Problems)

As we journey through the pages of globalization's historical chronicle, abstract ideas and theories often need to be distilled into more tangible stories. Let's pivot, then, to examine specific case studies that highlight both the benefits and the problems associated with globalization.

Our first case study takes us to the shores of the "Asian Tigers" – South Korea, Taiwan, Singapore, and Hong Kong. These countries achieved rapid industrialization and high growth rates from the 1960s to the 1990s. Capitalizing on open trade policies, strategic geographical locations, and a relentless focus on education, these countries transformed from agrarian economies into global powerhouses in sectors such as electronics, automobiles, and shipping. The Asian Tigers' story illustrates how a strategic embrace of globalization can lead to rapid economic development.

However, let's not forget the 1997 Asian Financial Crisis. The same forces of global integration that spurred growth also amplified risks. When the Thai baht collapsed, the crisis spread like wildfire across Asian economies, toppling currencies and creating economic havoc, demonstrating how globalization can transmit economic shocks across borders with alarming speed and intensity.

Now, let's hop on a plane to Africa, where we'll look at the impact of globalization on the textile industry in Lesotho. The implementation of the African Growth and Opportunity Act by the United States provided sub-Saharan African countries with duty-free access to American markets. This led to the burgeoning of a textile industry in Lesotho, which became the largest African exporter of garments to the U.S. This example demonstrates how globalization can create opportunities for sectors to flourish in unexpected places.

Meanwhile, over in North America, the story of NAFTA (North American Free Trade Agreement) unfolds. While it succeeded in tripling trade between Canada, the U.S., and Mexico, NAFTA also sparked controversies. Critics argue that it led to job losses in the U.S. as companies moved production to Mexico, where labor was cheaper. Proponents counter that it increased overall economic output. NAFTA exemplifies how the ramifications of trade agreements in a globalized world are complex and often contentious.

Finally, let's venture into the digital realm with the rise of Silicon Valley. This hub of technology and innovation owes much of its success to the free flow of ideas, people, and capital—facets central to globalization. Yet, this digital boom has also led to issues of privacy, misinformation, and a new kind of digital divide, exemplifying how the effects of globalization in the digital era are both empowering and problematic.

These case studies provide snapshots of globalization's multifaceted nature. They remind us that while globalization can act as a catalyst for economic growth and development, it can also exacerbate inequalities and transmit crises. It is a double-edged sword—its sharp blade can carve pathways to prosperity, but if mishandled, it can cut deep and leave lasting scars. As we navigate our way forward, it is crucial to learn from these case studies to harness the benefits of globalization while mitigating its potential downsides.

Chapter 2:
The Forces of Globalization

As we shift gears from the history of globalization, let's venture into the very engine room that powers this complex process - the forces of globalization. These forces - technological, economic, political, and social-cultural - are the pistons driving the machinery of globalization, shaping the contours of our interconnected world. In the ensuing sections, we will delve into each of these forces, exploring how they interrelate, amplify, and sometimes counteract each other. From the Internet's digital tendrils to the ebb and flow of global economies, from political agreements to cultural exchanges - we will explore how these forces continue to sculpt the landscape of our global society.

Technological Advances

If we could encapsulate one major driver of the global web we've spun, it would be technological advancement. Since the late 20th century, technology has dramatically accelerated the pace and scale of globalization, connecting every corner of our planet. It has redrafted how we communicate, trade, travel, and even think. This powerful propeller, however, did not always spin at such high speed.

In the early years of the last century, the invention of the telephone and the proliferation of railroads had already begun to weave together the threads of our global community. Trade and communication, though still slow and laborious by today's standards, saw significant improvements. The world began to shrink as information and goods traveled faster than ever before.

The real game-changer, however, arrived with the advent of the digital age. The development of the Internet marked a sea-change in the course of human civilization, bringing about unprecedented changes in the speed and manner in which we communicate. Never before had it been possible to connect with someone on the other side of the globe in real-time or share information instantaneously.

Meanwhile, transportation technology made leaps and bounds. The proliferation of air travel shrunk the world further, making it possible for people and goods to traverse great distances in hours instead of days or weeks. Containerization revolutionized trade by increasing the efficiency and volume of shipped goods, providing a boon to global commerce.

The digital revolution didn't stop at mere communication. It has also revolutionized manufacturing processes, logistics, and even how we conduct business, resulting in seamless global supply chains and new business models. The advent of Information Technology, the Internet of Things, Artificial Intelligence, and other advanced technologies have provided the scaffolding on which global networks have been built and continue to evolve.

The breakneck pace of technological advances in the 21st century continues to redefine the contours of globalization. The rise of digital platforms and cryptocurrencies, developments in AI and machine learning, breakthroughs in biotechnology, and advances in renewable energy technologies - all these and more continue to knit our world more tightly together.

However, the benefits of technological advancement are not without caveats. The digital divide between those with and without access to technology, issues of cybersecurity, and the impact of automation on jobs are just some of the challenges that have emerged alongside these advances. Balancing the immense potential of technological advancements with these pitfalls is an ongoing struggle in the narrative of globalization.

As we move forward, we stand on the brink of even greater technological breakthroughs, from quantum computing to revolutionary developments in space travel. There's no doubt that the relationship between technology and globalization will continue to evolve, continuing to redraw the map of our connected world.

Economic Drivers

As we traverse the labyrinth of factors that fuel globalization, one strand weaves its way more prominently than most others: the undeniable pull of economic forces. Like the pulse of a giant heart, the rhythm of global economic activity permeates every facet of our interconnected world, binding nations together in an intricate network of interdependencies.

To trace the tendrils of economic influence, we must start with the spread of capitalism. Emerging from the crucible of the Industrial Revolution, this economic system set the stage for modern globalization. Capitalism's inherent drive towards growth and expansion found fertile ground in the vast, uncharted territories beyond national borders. Thus began a dance of supply and demand on a global scale, a waltz of exchange and production that has grown in complexity over centuries.

In tandem with this, international trade has played an indispensable role as an economic driver. The allure of foreign markets, with their potential for higher profits and more diversified opportunities, has encouraged both competition and cooperation among nations. This economic exchange has further been facilitated by technological advances, as previously insurmountable geographical barriers gradually faded into irrelevance.

Multinational corporations, those gargantuan entities that straddle national boundaries, represent another cornerstone of economic globalization. Armed with vast resources and sophisticated technology, they navigate the channels of global trade, exploiting opportunities and creating new markets. They are the harbingers of foreign direct investment (FDI), transferring capital, technology, and expertise between nations, and thereby knitting together economies in a web of mutual benefit and dependency.

The liberalization of financial markets has further amplified the rate and reach of globalization. Capital now flows freely across borders, propelled by modern technological advancements that facilitate instantaneous transactions. From New York to Tokyo, London to Sydney, financial markets are interconnected in an intricate ballet of stocks, bonds, commodities, and currencies.

International institutions have played an instrumental role in shaping and facilitating these economic processes. The World Bank, International Monetary Fund, and the World Trade Organization, among others, have set the rules of the game, providing a framework within which global economic activities can operate.

Yet, just as with the tale of technology, the narrative of economic globalization has its share of shadows. The gap between the rich and the poor, both within and between nations, has widened. Unbridled capitalism has been criticized for promoting inequality, and the very mechanisms that drive global economic growth are often questioned for their environmental sustainability.

As we journey deeper into the 21st century, new economic landscapes emerge. The digital economy, green economy, and shared economy each present novel opportunities and challenges for globalization. The economic drivers of globalization are not static, but dynamic, evolving with the world they help shape. The challenge lies in harnessing these forces for the benefit of all, in the true spirit of a globally connected world.

Political Factors

As we wade through the torrent of global changes, the powerful undercurrent of political factors shaping globalization becomes increasingly evident. At first glance, politics and globalization may appear as separate entities - like dancers performing on opposite sides of the stage. However, their dance is more akin to a tango, each informing and influencing the other's moves with precision and nuance.

The very fabric of globalization is woven with threads of political decisions, negotiations, and conflicts. Domestic policies, international agreements, trade regulations, wars, and peace treaties - all these become threads that, when woven together, create the intricate tapestry of our global political and economic landscape. For instance, decisions on tariffs, subsidies, or immigration policy within a country can have far-reaching implications, rippling outwards and affecting global trade patterns, migration flows, and cultural exchanges.

Similarly, international agreements and organizations, such as the United Nations, the World Trade Organization, or regional trade blocs, play a vital role in shaping the contours of globalization. They set the rules of the game, determine how benefits and costs are distributed, and provide platforms for negotiation, conflict resolution, and cooperation. Without these political structures, globalization as we know it would be a vastly different beast, perhaps more feral and less predictable.

Moreover, globalization, with its flow of ideas, people, and goods, also feeds back into the political landscape. It brings new ideas and perspectives into the political arena, influences public opinion, shifts power dynamics, and even sparks social and political movements. Imagine a boomerang effect, where the very forces unleashed by political decisions return to reshape the political environment.

Yet, not all these political threads are woven evenly or equitably. Power asymmetries, both within and between countries, can lead to uneven patterns of globalization, where some countries and groups reap the benefits while others bear the costs. This is where the role of democracy, social movements, and civil society comes into play, providing checks and balances, advocating for equity, and giving voice to the marginalized.

Peeling back the layers, we also see how national politics and identities are shaped and reshaped by global forces. The rise of nationalism in some quarters, the debates around sovereignty, the political fault lines drawn around issues like climate change or immigration - all these are signposts of the intertwining dance of politics and globalization.

Politics, then, is not just a side player in the story of globalization; it's one of the main characters, often driving the plot and sometimes adding unexpected twists and turns. Just as in a thrilling dance performance, it's the push and pull, the interaction between the dancers - in this case, politics and globalization - that truly captivates and compels our attention. This dance is ongoing, and as the music of our changing world continues to play, we can expect political factors to continue playing a defining role in the rhythm of globalization.

Social and Cultural Factors

Picture yourself at a bustling bazaar, awash in a sea of sounds, sights, and scents from every corner of the world. The vibrant rhythm of diverse music, the colorful display of global fashion, the tantalizing aroma of a thousand different dishes — this sensory tapestry aptly symbolizes the impact of social and cultural factors in the narrative of globalization.

Just as a bazaar is a hub for the exchange of goods, the global stage serves as a platform for the exchange of ideas, values, traditions, and languages. These exchanges do not occur in a vacuum, but are deeply embedded within the social and cultural contexts from which they originate and into which they are introduced. As such, social and cultural factors have a profound and lasting impact on the course of globalization.

Migration, a social phenomenon as old as human history, has played an instrumental role in these exchanges. By moving across continents, countries, and cities, people carry their cultures, languages, traditions, and knowledge systems with them, facilitating cultural diffusion and the creation of multi-ethnic societies. As people intermingle, ideas and practices also intermingle, enriching the cultural milieu and fostering innovation and creativity.

Simultaneously, technological advances have created virtual bridges between cultures and societies. From social media platforms to online communities, technology has not only made the world smaller, but has also facilitated an unprecedented level of intercultural communication and learning. The ripple effects of this digital democratization of information and interaction are felt across multiple dimensions of society — from education and business to entertainment and activism.

However, the interplay of social and cultural factors and globalization is not always harmonious. The dominance of Western cultures, particularly in the realms of media and popular culture, raises concerns about cultural imperialism and the erosion of local cultures and languages. In response, there have been concerted efforts to protect and preserve cultural diversity and heritage, as well as to foster a more inclusive and equitable dialogue among cultures.

Moreover, social inequality can affect the pace and pattern of globalization. Access to technological advances, quality education, and economic opportunities is not evenly distributed, leading to a digital divide and perpetuating social inequalities on a global scale. This is where the role of social movements, civil society, and inclusive policies becomes vital in addressing these inequities and ensuring that the fruits of globalization are shared more equitably.

Indeed, the globalization saga is as much about the diffusion of cultures and the reshaping of social landscapes as it is about the flow of goods, services, and capital. The social and cultural threads intricately woven into this saga add richness and complexity to our understanding of globalization. As the bazaar of globalization continues to hum with activity, it is these social and cultural exchanges, dialogues, and conflicts that will continue to shape its contour and character.

Chapter 3:
The Impact of Globalization

In a world increasingly entwined by the threads of global interactions, we find ourselves part of an interconnected tapestry, woven from the loom of globalization. In this chapter, we will navigate the intricate patterns of this tapestry, exploring how globalization shapes our economies, drives political alliances and contentions, affects the environment, and moulds our cultural norms and practices. From the ebb and flow of global economies to the struggle for environmental sustainability, from the powerful political currents to the cultural exchange - this chapter will take you through an enriching journey of understanding the profound impact of globalization. We shall examine each thread of this intricate fabric, bringing us closer to understanding our connected world. So, let's embark on this journey to comprehend the multi-dimensional impacts of globalization, shall we?

Global Economy

Welcome to the great bazaar, the bustling marketplace of the world, where goods, services, and currencies whirl in a ceaseless dance of exchange. This grand spectacle is the Global Economy, a key aspect of globalization, wherein every transaction, every deal, and every trade agreement can trigger a ripple effect that traverses continents.

The Global Economy operates on the principles of interdependence and integration, powered by the invisible hands of supply and demand. Countries trade with each other, resulting in a complex web of economic relations. It is akin to a vast orchestra where every nation plays its own economic instrument. One country's increased productivity can trigger another's industrial growth, demonstrating the symphony of the global economy.

As with any good show, there are both stars and supporting actors. Developed nations often take center stage with their robust economies and influential multinational corporations. These countries wield considerable power in setting the economic tempo of the world. But let's not forget the emerging economies. Like understudies waiting in the wings, these nations are rapidly gaining momentum, contributing significantly to the global economic landscape.

Of course, in this grand performance of the global economy, free trade is the maestro. It orchestrates the movements of goods and services across borders, with trade agreements serving as the sheet music. Free trade agreements have indeed played a pivotal role in fueling economic globalization, promoting increased economic cooperation and competition.

However, the global economy isn't all bright lights and applause. It has its own set of challenges, notably economic disparity and volatility. Unequal distribution of wealth is a persistent issue, with wealth concentrated in certain countries or within specific segments of populations. Additionally, economic crises in one country can quickly ripple through the global economy, demonstrating the interconnected nature of our world but also highlighting its susceptibility to instability.

Moreover, globalization has ushered in an era of transnational corporations. These enterprises, operating in multiple countries simultaneously, wield substantial economic influence. They can drive job growth, impact trade balances, and even sway political decisions. However, their reach and power also raise concerns about economic sovereignty and local economic stability.

In the end, the global economy is a compelling act in the drama of globalization. It is a stage where opportunities for growth and prosperity coexist with challenges of disparity and volatility. The key, as always, is to strive for balance, ensuring that the global economic dance continues to be a waltz of prosperity, not a tango of disparity. It's a delicate dance, but one that we must continue to master in our connected world.

Global Politics

Picture a vast chessboard that spans continents, with players positioned across every corner of the globe. Welcome to the complex, intricate game of Global Politics. In this arena, nations navigate their way through strategic alliances, power tussles, and policy negotiations, each maneuver influencing the game's dynamics. This game is an integral part of globalization, for politics and globalization are intricately entwined, each shaping the contours of the other.

Global Politics operates in an intricate tapestry of interconnected relationships and influences, powered by the dual engines of cooperation and conflict. Nations form alliances, engage in diplomatic negotiations, establish treaties, and sometimes clash in conflicts, painting a rich, dynamic tableau of global interactions. Much like a grand theatre play, each act has a rippling impact, influencing global policies, international relations, and world events.

Supranational entities play a significant role in this game, setting the stage for cooperation, arbitration, and governance on a global scale. Bodies like the United Nations, the World

Bank, and the International Monetary Fund represent these key players. Their decisions and policies shape economic, social, and political landscapes, highlighting the intricate link between globalization and politics.

Simultaneously, soft power – a country's cultural influence, diplomatic finesse, and global perception – acts as a subtle yet potent tool in global politics. Countries wield their soft power to influence diplomatic outcomes, win allies, and carve a favorable image on the global stage.

However, the game of global politics is not without its challenges. Sovereignty, a country's ability to govern itself without external interference, often comes under strain in an increasingly interconnected world. Balancing national interests with global obligations, managing conflicts, addressing human rights issues, and navigating the effects of economic interdependence are other prominent challenges in global politics.

The game gets even more complex with the advent of digital technology. Cyber warfare, information manipulation, and digital diplomacy add new dimensions to global politics, redefining power dynamics and raising pressing issues about digital governance and cybersecurity.

At the end of the day, global politics is a fascinating, albeit complex, aspect of globalization. It's a game that requires diplomatic finesse, strategic acumen, and a keen understanding of global dynamics. The actors on this stage wield considerable influence in shaping our interconnected world, underlining the importance of political wisdom, tact, and foresight in navigating the intricate dance of global politics.

Environment and Sustainability

Picture our planet as a vast jigsaw puzzle where every piece, be it a butterfly in the Amazon rainforest or a droplet in the Arctic Ocean, holds significance. Globalization, in all its ubiquity, has rearranged this puzzle in countless ways, leaving a profound impact on the environment and sustainability. As we navigate through the 21st century, understanding this relationship becomes increasingly crucial for the survival and prosperity of our interconnected world.

One of the key environmental impacts of globalization stems from the intensified exploitation of natural resources. As trade barriers drop and markets open, the demand for raw materials skyrockets. Forests shrink, mines deepen, and oceans are overfished to quench the world's burgeoning appetite for goods. This rampant consumption, driven by globalization, strains the planet's resources, leading to significant environmental degradation.

Closely related to resource exploitation is pollution. With increased industrialization and mass production, waste generation has reached unprecedented levels. From the smog-filled air in metropolises to plastic-choked oceans, pollution is a stark testament to globalization's darker side. Climate change, arguably the most pressing issue of our time, is intrinsically tied to this problem. Fossil fuel use, deforestation, and industrial processes contribute massively to greenhouse gas emissions, exacerbating global warming and extreme weather events.

Yet, it isn't all doom and gloom. Globalization also holds potential for positive change. The sharing of knowledge, technology, and resources across borders can foster sustainable development. Renewable energy technologies, for instance, are being adopted globally, reducing dependency on fossil fuels. Cross-border cooperation, exemplified by international treaties like the Paris Agreement, shows our collective resolve to tackle environmental issues.

Moreover, the interconnectedness of our world has amplified voices calling for sustainable practices. Grassroots movements, non-profit organizations, and even businesses are increasingly advocating for greener practices, transforming the global discourse around sustainability. As these voices echo louder in the global amphitheater, the demand for sustainable, ethical, and eco-friendly products and services is rising, encouraging corporations to embed sustainability into their core business strategies.

On the flip side, a crucial challenge is ensuring that the benefits of sustainable practices are equitably distributed. There's a danger of widening the socio-economic gap, as poorer countries may lack the resources or technology to adapt to greener practices as quickly as their wealthier counterparts.

At the heart of it, Environment and Sustainability is a balancing act in the arena of globalization. As stewards of this interconnected world, our challenge lies in leveraging the benefits of globalization while mitigating its adverse impacts on the environment. We must remember, every jigsaw piece matters, and our collective actions will shape the image that finally emerges on the puzzle board of our planet.

Culture and Society

Imagine a global dance floor, where rhythms from every corner of the world intertwine, creating a unique blend of melodies. That, my friends, is the cultural and societal impact of globalization. This synergistic dance has redefined our collective identity, as ideas, beliefs, traditions, and social norms now cross borders as easily as the latest international news update.

Globalization has allowed cultures to spread and intermingle in unprecedented ways. For instance, foods, once considered exotic, have found homes in foreign lands, adding new flavors to local cuisines. Japanese sushi can now be enjoyed in downtown Denver, while a foodie in Tokyo might savor the spicy kick of Mexican enchiladas.

The film and music industries, too, have been dramatically reshaped. Bollywood films play to packed houses in London, and Korean pop music, or K-pop, is all the rage from Seoul to São Paulo. This cultural fusion has enriched our global entertainment, creating a multicultural medley that speaks to our shared human experience.

Technology, particularly the Internet, has amplified this cultural exchange. Social media platforms allow for instantaneous sharing of ideas and trends, making them powerful engines of cultural transmission. The viral nature of internet trends exemplifies how local cultural expressions can quickly become global phenomena.

In this interconnected world, societies are also converging on certain shared values. Concepts such as human rights, gender equality, and environmental responsibility are gaining universal recognition. With a global stage, advocates can rally support for these issues, leveraging the power of international consensus to catalyze change.

However, the impacts of globalization on culture and society are not all rosy. Critics argue that it can lead to cultural homogenization or 'Westernization,' where dominant cultures overpower and eclipse local traditions. The proliferation of American fast food outlets around the world, sometimes at the expense of local eateries, is often cited as an example of this.

Globalization can also exacerbate social inequalities, both within and between countries. As wealth and resources flow across borders, they often land in the pockets of those already well-off, widening the chasm between the haves and the have-nots.

While it is essential to recognize these concerns, let's not forget the compelling side of the story. The cultural interactions brought about by globalization, despite their complexities, offer an incredible opportunity for mutual understanding and social progression.

As we dance to the tunes of this global symphony, it is up to us to ensure that every beat—every culture, every society— has the chance to contribute to the melody. In the grand dance of globalization, we must respect and value the diverse rhythms that make the music so rich and harmonious. After all, it is in this cultural confluence that we find the true essence of our connected world.

Chapter 4: Globalization in Different Regions

Picture a shimmering, multifaceted gemstone. Each facet of this gem represents a distinct region of our planet, and just like the varying hues and angles of light within the gemstone, globalization has impacted each region in its unique way. In this chapter, we delve into the specific impacts and character of globalization in North America, Europe, Asia, Africa, and Latin America. We will examine how globalization's intricate dance has influenced the economic, political, social, and cultural landscapes of these regions. Whether it's the innovation-driving economies of North America, the unified yet diverse landscape of Europe, the fast-growing powerhouses in Asia, the rich cultural tapestry of Africa, or the vibrant blend of tradition and transformation in Latin America, we'll discover that while globalization may be a global phenomenon, its impacts are deeply local and unique. So, let's embark on this journey, shedding light on the distinct contours of our gemstone, illuminating the fascinating nuances of our connected world.

Globalization in North America

Picture a sprinter in the starting blocks, muscles tense, ready to leap forward with the crack of the starter's pistol. That's an apt metaphor for North America at the dawn of the globalization era. As one of the engines of globalization, North America – primarily represented by the United States and Canada – launched into the globalized world with a head start, shaping and being shaped by the process.

The intertwined threads of technological innovation and economic power have made North America a central player in globalization. Its tech companies and startups, from Silicon Valley to Seattle, have transformed the world's digital landscape, fostering connections that span the globe. The impact has been transformative, disrupting traditional industries and generating entirely new ones, from social media to remote work platforms.

The region has also played a vital role in constructing the infrastructure of globalization. North American corporations have extended their influence overseas, driving investment, creating employment, and fostering cultural exchange. Yet this economic powerhouse status has its downsides. There's been a significant outflow of manufacturing jobs to countries where labor is cheaper, creating pockets of economic distress in some North American communities.

Politically, North America's approach to international cooperation has shaped global norms and institutions. The United Nations headquarters in New York, international financial institutions like the International Monetary Fund, and other such entities owe their existence in part to North American political influence.

Yet, it's not just a one-way street. International events and trends have significantly impacted North American domestic policies and politics. Issues such as immigration, trade disputes, and transnational terrorism have been sources of intense political debate and policy realignments.

On a societal level, North America's cultures are a living testament to globalization. A kaleidoscope of languages, religions, and traditions coexist, creating vibrant, diverse societies. The constant flow of people, ideas, and cultural practices has led to an ever-evolving cultural landscape, influenced by global trends, yet uniquely North American.

However, as with all aspects of globalization, there are complexities. The increasing diversity has occasionally led to tensions, as different cultures grapple with cohabitation and integration. Additionally, the global media's influence on societal norms and values has stirred debates about cultural homogenization.

In essence, North America's experience with globalization is a dynamic interplay of global influence and regional characteristics. As we move forward, it's crucial to consider how this interplay will shape North America's future in our increasingly interconnected world.

Globalization in Europe

Imagine a grand old dame, rich in culture and history, yet capable of keeping pace with the vivacity of modern times. That's Europe in the context of globalization. As one of the oldest cradles of civilization, Europe presents a unique case study in how a region steeped in tradition adapts to a rapidly globalizing world.

Technological advances have enabled European nations to maintain their competitiveness in the global market. The region has been a hub for scientific research and innovation, with a robust presence in industries ranging from automobile manufacturing to renewable energy. Companies like BMW, Siemens, and ABB are testament to Europe's technological prowess and its global influence.

Economically, Europe has been a leader in globalization. The formation of the European Union and the adoption of a single currency, the Euro, stand as symbols of regional economic integration unprecedented in scale. This integration has facilitated intra-European trade, attracting foreign investments and creating a significant player in global trade. However, the economic integration has also come with challenges, such as disparities in economic growth and wealth distribution among member states, not to mention the ongoing conversations about financial responsibility and sovereignty.

Politically, Europe has had an essential role in establishing and leading international organizations, including the United Nations and NATO. The advocacy for democracy, human rights, and rule of law in the international arena has been shaped significantly by European values and norms.

However, the influx of immigrants and refugees, driven by global crises, has challenged the region's political stability. It has sparked intense debates on immigration policy, national identity, and social integration. The rise of far-right political movements in some countries, often fueled by anti-globalization sentiment, is a stark reminder of the complex interplay between globalization and politics.

Culturally, Europe is a mosaic, where ancient cathedrals coexist with modern skyscrapers, and traditional practices mingle with global trends. The impact of globalization on this cultural tapestry has been both enriching and contentious. On one hand, globalization has led to an explosion of cultural exchange, introducing new foods, music, and ideas. On the other hand, concerns about the erosion of local cultures and languages have led to the rise of cultural preservation movements.

In many ways, Europe embodies the complexity of globalization. It's a vibrant and diverse region grappling with the challenges of maintaining unity while celebrating diversity, of balancing economic growth with social equality, and of preserving rich traditions in the face of a rapidly changing world. Understanding Europe's journey through globalization provides a valuable lens into the opportunities and challenges that come with our interconnected world.

Globalization in Asia

The story of globalization in Asia is a tale of transformation. It's a journey that sees a continent of diverse cultures and histories, bridging the gap between ancient traditions and cutting-edge technology, becoming the world's fastest-growing economic region. This section delves into the multiple facets of globalization in Asia - technologically, economically, politically, and culturally.

Technology in Asia runs the gamut from China's global tech titans like Alibaba and Tencent to India's vibrant IT services and software development industry. South Korea's tech behemoth Samsung and Japan's Sony stand tall in electronics. Asia has embraced the digital revolution, which has permeated everyday life, from online shopping to digital payments, leading to unprecedented internet penetration rates and digital literacy.

On the economic front, Asia's economic powerhouses, Japan and China, stand side by side with fast-growing economies like India, Vietnam, and Indonesia. Asia's position as a global manufacturing hub, marked by China's ascendance as the "world's factory," has been pivotal to the globalization process. Besides, the burgeoning middle class across the region is a beacon for global marketers. Yet, income disparity and socio-economic inequality remain significant challenges amid this breakneck economic growth.

In terms of politics, Asia's role in global geopolitics has escalated alongside its economic rise. The shifting dynamics between the U.S. and China, often referred to as the Thucydides Trap, and its ripple effects in the South China Sea dispute, North Korea's nuclear ambitions, or India and China's border tensions, showcase the complex political undercurrents shaping Asia in a global context. At the same time, regional alliances like ASEAN reflect the collective strength and cooperative spirit in this part of the world.

Culturally, Asia is a vibrant collage of languages, religions, cuisines, and art forms. Globalization has spurred a wave of cultural exchange, with Asian pop culture, like K-pop or Bollywood movies, finding global audiences. Simultaneously, western lifestyle and entertainment have found their way into Asian societies. This interchange, while enriching, has also sparked concerns about cultural homogenization and loss of local traditions.

Ecologically, Asia is grappling with the repercussions of rapid industrialization and urbanization. From air pollution in India and China to deforestation in Southeast Asia, environmental issues have come to the forefront. Globalization has driven the need for pan-Asian collaboration on climate change mitigation and sustainable practices, like in the Paris Agreement.

The journey of globalization in Asia is ongoing, vibrant, and sometimes contentious. It's a tale of extraordinary growth, technological progress, and cultural intermingling but also a story of grappling with the socio-economic disparity, political tension, and environmental challenges. Through the Asian lens, one can glean valuable insights into the multi-faceted impacts of globalization.

Globalization in Africa

In understanding globalization, the African continent provides a compelling backdrop, where the melding of tradition and innovation, the push and pull of local and global forces, paint a complex, vibrant, and poignant tableau. In this section, we examine the imprint of globalization in Africa, charting its trajectory across technology, economy, politics, culture, and environment.

Technologically, Africa has made significant strides, largely leapfrogging the intermediary steps witnessed in other regions. Mobile technology, for example, is a game-changer in Africa, providing a wide range of services, from banking to health care, often in areas where traditional infrastructure is lacking. Consider M-Pesa, Kenya's mobile money service, a shining example of innovative solutions tailored to local needs.

Economically, globalization has reshaped Africa's role in the global marketplace. It is no longer just a supplier of raw materials but also an emerging market with increasing consumer power. Chinese investment in Africa underscores this shift, spanning infrastructure projects, manufacturing, and services. However, Africa's relationship with the global economy is nuanced, with criticisms of neo-colonialism, unfair trade practices, and the perpetuation of economic disparities.

Politically, African nations have grown more integrated into the global stage, with African Union, an embodiment of this shift. Yet, it's a challenging journey marred by governance issues, corruption, and conflicts. Globalization has both played a role in exacerbating some of these issues and offered tools to combat them, such as through international human rights advocacy and peacekeeping efforts.

Culturally, Africa's rich tapestry of traditions has found a global stage, from Afrobeat music to African literature, garnering worldwide recognition and appreciation. Yet, this cultural export comes with concerns about cultural appropriation and the risk of losing local cultural identity in the face of Western influences.

Environmentally, Africa is at the frontline of global climate change despite contributing the least to greenhouse gas emissions. From droughts in East Africa to flooding in Mozambique, the impacts of climate change pose significant challenges. Globalization, while contributing to these issues, also offers avenues for solutions, such as international climate accords and green technology transfer.

As we explore globalization in Africa, we encounter a narrative of transformation, ingenuity, but also challenge. From tech-savvy youth, burgeoning markets, and rich cultural export to economic imbalances, political upheavals, and environmental challenges, Africa's experience with globalization is a prism reflecting the intricate interplay of global forces. It is a journey of resilience, adaptation, and a continuous quest for equitable development in an interconnected world.

Globalization in Latin America

Globalization's trajectory in Latin America is a vivid tapestry of vast potential, stark realities, heartening triumphs, and sobering challenges. The region's journey with globalization is a tale of the tango between tradition and modernity, between local dynamics and global forces. We delve into this intricate dance across the arenas of technology, economy, politics, culture, and the environment.

In the realm of technology, Latin America has witnessed transformative change, enabling greater connectivity and fostering innovation. This surge in technology adoption, spurred in large part by mobile and internet penetration, has bridged distances, enhanced information exchange, and provided new opportunities. Yet, the digital divide and uneven access to these technological advancements remain pressing concerns.

From an economic perspective, globalization has made Latin America a pivotal player in the global market, particularly in sectors like agriculture and mining. The region has been the beneficiary of foreign investment and trade agreements that have boosted exports. However, it also grapples with economic dependency, commodity boom-and-bust cycles, and inequality. Debt crises and the effects of economic liberalization policies serve as sober reminders of the complexities entwined with globalization.

Politically, Latin America's engagement with globalization is marked by a shift towards democratic governance and increased participation in international institutions. Yet, political instability, corruption, and social unrest are enduring challenges. The tug-of-war between neoliberal policies and populist movements is a recurring theme, underscoring the intricate interplay of domestic politics and globalization.

Culturally, Latin American music, literature, film, and art have gained worldwide acclaim, bolstered by the forces of globalization. This cultural flowering, however, is twofold. On the one hand, it offers global exposure to Latin American cultures; on the other, it raises questions about cultural homogenization and the erosion of local identities.

Environmentally, Latin America faces a complex conundrum. Home to the Amazon rainforest, the 'lungs of the Earth', the region is a key stakeholder in global environmental sustainability. Yet, pressures from global demands for commodities risk compromising its diverse ecosystems. The interconnection of local practices and global consumption patterns lays bare the environmental implications of globalization.

Our journey through Latin America's experience with globalization takes us through a dynamic landscape of change, growth, struggle, and resilience. The region's saga with globalization is a reflection of its spirited tango, a dance marked by elegant strides, abrupt turns, and fervent passion - a dance that continues to evolve in rhythm with the global symphony.

Chapter 5:
Globalization and Development

S trap in for an exciting journey as we venture into the multifaceted realm of globalization and development. We shall explore globalization's myriad effects on different categories of nations - the developed, the developing, and the least developed. This chapter delves into the transformations and tribulations that have unfolded in these countries in their interaction with globalization. From the skyscraper-studded cities of developed nations to the bustling markets of developing economies, and the resilient communities in the least developed countries, we traverse a spectrum of realities. We will examine how globalization has played a role in shaping economic structures, political landscapes, social fabrics, and environmental prospects in these diverse contexts. It's time to dust off the passport of your imagination, for we are embarking on a globe-spanning journey through the complex terrain of globalization and development.

Impact on Developed Nations

Globalization, like a talented conductor leading an orchestra, has directed a symphony of transformation across developed nations. The journey has not always been harmonious, but the score has changed irrevocably.

In terms of economic impact, globalization has been a vigorous catalyst. Through the growth of trade and international investments, it has amplified economic expansion, facilitated wealth accumulation, and stimulated technological innovation. Many developed nations have outsourced manufacturing to cheaper labor markets, allowing them to shift towards a service-oriented economy. This shift has not been without its discordant notes, particularly for those in industries now largely offshored, but the overall melody, the trend line, points to an increase in living standards for a significant majority.

On the social front, globalization has acted as a bridge, connecting disparate cultures, fostering understanding, and spawning an environment of multiculturalism and diversity. The exchange of ideas, values, and knowledge has enriched societies, opening minds to new concepts and perspectives. However, we can't ignore the cacophonous chords, with some individuals feeling alienated in their own society due to rapid changes, or disillusioned by the perceived loss of traditional cultural identity.

In the realm of politics, the song of globalization carries themes of international cooperation and diplomacy. Developed nations have seen an increased role in international institutions and global governance structures, their policies often echoing in the corridors of the United Nations, the World Trade Organization, and other international bodies. However, it's important to note the tensions globalization can cause, as nations juggle between domestic demands and international expectations.

Environmentally, developed nations have been both performers and spectators in the symphony of globalization. On one hand, they have been pioneers in championing sustainable development and ecological initiatives on the global stage. Conversely, the high consumption habits powered by globalization have led to increased resource extraction, pollution, and environmental degradation.

As we dissect the impact of globalization on developed nations, we must keep in mind that this is an ongoing composition, a symphony yet to reach its finale. The ebbs and flows, crescendos and diminuendos, the harmonious melodies and jarring dissonances, all contribute to a complex and evolving masterpiece. And remember, while we as audience members may have our opinions on the performance so far, it is the nations themselves who hold the baton, and the power to influence the final notes of their own orchestral piece.

Impact on Developing Nations

Globalization, with its chameleonic nature, has painted an interesting, though often complex, picture in developing nations. The strokes of this global paintbrush have brought vibrant hues of prosperity and promise, but also shades of uncertainty and challenge.

Consider the economic palette. The infusion of foreign capital, the liberalization of trade, and the opening of markets have all created a kaleidoscope of opportunities for economic growth. By allowing access to larger consumer bases and the provision of cheaper goods and services, globalization has generated jobs and increased income levels. However, it hasn't been all sunshine and roses. Some sectors, unable to compete with foreign competition, have struggled or even vanished. Additionally, dependency on volatile global markets can lead to a precarious economic balance.

Socially, globalization has introduced developing nations to a variety of cultures, promoting diversity and inclusivity. Exposure to different ways of life has led to societal transformation, empowering individuals with broader perspectives. However, it's not always been a harmonious fusion. The rapid pace of change can result in the erosion of local cultures, creating a mélange of hybrid identities that may lead to social tension and dislocation.

The political domain has witnessed a medley of influences due to globalization. Participation in international institutions and agreements has enhanced diplomatic relations, promoting peace and collaboration. But, at times, these international norms and standards may seem to infringe on national sovereignty, triggering resistance and generating discord.

From an environmental perspective, developing nations are at a crossroads. Globalization has propelled them into the industrial age, accelerating development but also intensifying pollution and resource degradation. The struggle here is between the urgent need for growth and the vital necessity for sustainability, a delicate balancing act on a global tightrope.

In summary, the impact of globalization on developing nations is a rich tapestry of contrasts, a mix of gains and losses, opportunities and challenges. The trick is to appreciate the artwork in its entirety – the bright colors and the dark shades – and strive for a balance that best serves the interests of these nations. Globalization can be a potent medium for transformation and growth, but it requires skilled artisans who can effectively navigate its intricacies and idiosyncrasies. In the hands of such master craftsmen, the potential benefits for developing nations can indeed be vast.

Impact on Least Developed Countries

The winds of globalization have blown through the landscapes of the world's least developed countries (LDCs), and the effect has been like a hot air balloon ride:

breathtaking vistas interspersed with heart-stopping plunges. This section of our journey through the globalization narrative invites us to explore the layered impacts this phenomenon has had on the world's most vulnerable nations.

The economic sphere presents a picture of contrasts. On one hand, globalized markets have offered these countries wider access to trade and investment, opening doors to potential prosperity. Small as these economies might be, the global platform has allowed them to showcase their unique products, from exotic spices to hand-woven fabrics. On the other hand, they find themselves in the challenging position of competing with more developed economies, often leading to an economic game of snakes and ladders, where progress can be painfully slow and setbacks swift.

In terms of social aspects, the impact of globalization has been akin to an interesting novel, filled with fascinating characters and intriguing plot twists. Exposure to global cultures has expanded horizons, altering perceptions and instigating social change. Yet, the fast pace of this change can strain the social fabric, resulting in the displacement of indigenous cultures and traditions. It's as if these nations are in a dance with globalization, where the steps are unfamiliar and the rhythm can be dizzyingly fast.

When it comes to politics, globalization has been both a protagonist and an antagonist. LDCs have been able to form alliances, find their voices in international forums, and leverage global norms for national benefit. But sometimes, the external pressure to comply with these norms can undermine local autonomy, creating a subplot of resistance and conflict.

Environmentally, globalization presents an urgent conundrum for LDCs. The race to develop can lead to unsustainable practices, exacerbating environmental degradation and contributing to global issues like climate change. It's like being caught in a whirlwind, where the rush to move forward stirs up a storm of problems.

In essence, the impact of globalization on the least developed countries is a multifaceted story, brimming with opportunities and fraught with challenges. It's a narrative of transformation, where the plot is complex and the characters dynamic. The task for these nations is to navigate the plot twists and character developments in a way that moves their story towards a happy ending. The hope is that they can turn the page on poverty and hardship and write a new chapter of sustainable growth and prosperity.

Chapter 6:
Key Institutions in Globalization

Diving into the chapter of "Key Institutions in Globalization," we'll be meeting the heavy-hitters of our global story, the organizations that act as the conductors orchestrating the symphony of worldwide interconnectivity. From the diplomatic powerhouse of the United Nations, to the financial behemoths that are the World Bank and IMF, to the global marketplace director, the World Trade Organization, and finally the various regional trading blocs and economic unions, each plays a unique role in this grand opera. Through the coming sections, we'll explore their roles, their impacts, their achievements, and the controversies that surround them, illuminating the backstage operations that shape our global stage. So grab your playbill, and let's prepare to watch these institutions in action.

The Role of the United Nations

Picture a global town hall meeting, where 193 countries are gathered around one figurative table, each with their own interests, cultures, and challenges. That is the United Nations - an arena where nations come together to maintain international peace and security, promote sustainable development, protect human rights, uphold international law, and deliver humanitarian aid. In our interconnected world, the UN's role has expanded and evolved to address complex, global challenges that cannot be solved by one nation alone.

The UN's origin story began with the grim aftermath of World War II, when global leaders decided that a cooperative international framework was crucial to prevent another large-scale conflict. Since then, the UN has made significant contributions in maintaining peace through conflict resolution and peacekeeping missions. It has been instrumental in averting full-blown wars, mediating peace agreements, and rebuilding societies shattered by conflicts.

In terms of global development, the UN has been a forerunner in setting agendas and goals. The Millennium Development Goals (MDGs) and Sustainable Development Goals (SDGs) are prime examples of this. These initiatives have prompted countries to work on universal challenges such as poverty, education, gender equality, climate change, and more.

Yet, the UN's role is not confined to negotiation tables or high-level forums. Its humanitarian work is equally profound. UN agencies like the World Food Programme (WFP), the United Nations Children's Fund (UNICEF), and the World Health Organization (WHO) provide emergency assistance, long-term aid, and health services to millions of people around the globe. These organizations are the safety nets that catch those who fall through the cracks of global development.

Moreover, the UN is an important custodian of international law. Its conventions, treaties, and standards form a critical part of the international legal framework that governs everything from maritime laws to human rights, from climate agreements to disarmament.

But for all its commendable roles, the United Nations is not without its fair share of criticisms. Its decision-making structure, particularly the power wielded by the permanent members of the Security Council, has been a contentious issue. Questions have been raised about its effectiveness in preventing conflicts, its accountability, and the need for it to adapt to the changing dynamics of the 21st century.

In the final analysis, the UN is an indispensable actor in the story of globalization. It symbolizes our collective aspirations for a peaceful and equitable world, our shared endeavors to achieve them, and the intricate challenges that come along the way. As the world continues to grapple with a plethora of issues, the United Nations' role in harmonizing global efforts is more crucial than ever. As we move forward, we must continue to scrutinize its roles, celebrate its successes, and constructively address its shortcomings.

The Role of the World Bank and IMF

Once upon a time, in the aftermath of the Second World War, two towering institutions were born, whose influence would touch every corner of the globe. These twins, the International Monetary Fund (IMF) and the World Bank, were to become pivotal in the tale of globalization, each playing unique yet interlinked roles in the global economy.

The IMF came to life with the chief purpose of promoting international monetary cooperation, ensuring exchange rate stability, and providing short-term monetary support to countries that encountered balance of payments difficulties. With its expertise in financial surveillance and policy advice, the IMF has helped maintain stability in the international monetary system and prevent economic crises.

Yet, it's not all about crisis management for the IMF. The Fund has been instrumental in offering technical assistance and training to help countries build better economic institutions and strengthen their policy-making capacity. In short, it's like having an experienced financial advisor on a global scale, giving advice and support during both sunny and stormy economic weathers.

In parallel, the World Bank, composed primarily of the International Bank for Reconstruction and Development (IBRD) and the International Development Association (IDA), has been busy playing its part in the story. The World Bank focuses more on longer-term economic development and poverty reduction. By providing loans and grants for a broad array of development activities, ranging from infrastructure projects to education and healthcare initiatives, it aims to lift the living standards in developing countries.

Moreover, the World Bank is not just a lender, but also a hub for knowledge and research. Its reports and data resources provide important insights into various aspects of global development and play a significant role in shaping development discourse and policies.

However, it's important to note that these institutions are not just financial wizards sprinkling fairy dust of prosperity everywhere. They have been at the center of controversies and criticisms. Some criticize their conditionality on loans, which often require structural adjustment policies involving austerity measures and market liberalization, arguing that these can lead to negative social impacts. Others point out the disproportionate voting power of the richer countries, raising concerns about fairness and representation.

Nonetheless, their contributions to the narrative of globalization cannot be overlooked. From post-war reconstruction, managing financial crises, to promoting sustainable development, the IMF and World Bank have helped write the script of the global economic order. As we flip to the future chapters of globalization, it's crucial that we continue to assess their roles and encourage reforms to make them more effective, inclusive, and accountable.

The Role of the World Trade Organization

In the bustling marketplace of global trade, if countries were shopkeepers and international trade the vast bazaar, then the World Trade Organization (WTO) would be the custodian, the rules-maker, the judge, and the facilitator. Born in 1995 out of the ashes of the General Agreement on Tariffs and Trade (GATT), the WTO stepped onto the world stage with a mission to promote free trade, ensure predictable trade relations, and resolve trade disputes.

The WTO operates on a set of core principles that guide global trade. Most notably, these include non-discrimination, which emphasizes that each member should treat all other members equally, and reciprocity, which encourages countries to engage in mutual trade concessions. These principles act as a common playbook for trade, providing certainty and predictability to global commerce.

As a forum for trade negotiations, the WTO is the venue where member countries thrash out the terms of trade agreements. It oversees a comprehensive body of trade agreements, covering goods, services, and intellectual property rights. The scope of its mandate is expansive, touching upon areas such as agriculture, textiles, banking, telecommunications, and even environmental issues as they relate to trade.

Moreover, the WTO has an important role as a referee in global trade disputes. Its Dispute Settlement Body provides a structured mechanism for resolving conflicts, helping members to avoid trade wars that could have significant impacts on the global economy. In essence, it is like a referee in the vast football field of global trade, blowing the whistle when players foul and ensuring everyone sticks to the rules.

However, while it champions free trade, the WTO is not without its critics. Some argue that the principle of consensus in decision-making makes progress difficult, leading to the so-called "Doha Round" negotiations dragging on for years. Others criticize the WTO for perpetuating inequality, asserting that it often favors the interests of developed countries and multinational corporations over those of developing nations.

Despite these challenges, the WTO remains a crucial actor in the theatre of globalization. It continues to shape the course of international trade, making it more orderly and predictable. As we navigate the future of globalization, we need to engage in continuous dialogue on how to improve the WTO and make it a more effective and equitable institution in the rapidly changing global economy.

Regional Trading Blocs and Economic Unions

As the world has become more connected, some nations have found strength in unity. Regional trading blocs and economic unions have risen as powerful figures on the chessboard of globalization. They represent a desire for collective progress and shared prosperity, providing a framework for economic collaboration between countries that are geographically proximate and often share similar political or economic objectives.

Regional trading blocs, such as the North American Free Trade Agreement (NAFTA), the Association of Southeast Asian Nations (ASEAN), and the Southern Common Market (MERCOSUR), facilitate trade between member countries by reducing or eliminating tariffs and import quotas. The result is an increase in economic activity, as goods flow more freely across borders. These blocs create larger markets for businesses within their jurisdictions, leading to economies of scale and greater competitiveness on a global scale.

Meanwhile, economic unions take collaboration a step further by adopting common economic policies. The most prominent example of this is the European Union (EU), a unique economic and political union of 27 European countries. The EU boasts a single market where goods, services, capital, and people move freely, bolstered by a shared currency—the Euro—used by 19 of its member states. This integrated approach not only strengthens economic ties but also fosters political cooperation and cultural understanding among member nations.

The emergence of regional trading blocs and economic unions has significantly altered the global economic landscape. They influence global trade patterns, negotiating trade agreements as a unified entity rather than individual nations. By doing so, these unions wield significant power in setting international trade standards and regulations.

Yet, like most things under the sun, they come with their share of controversies. Critics argue that these blocs create a sense of economic nationalism, favoring trade within the bloc over trade with the rest of the world—an aspect that can be seen as contrary to the broader philosophy of free trade. Additionally, while member countries might benefit from increased trade and cooperation, these benefits are not always evenly distributed, potentially leading to economic and social disparities within the bloc or union.

In the grand scheme of globalization, regional trading blocs and economic unions represent an interesting paradox. They embody the spirit of economic integration while simultaneously fortifying regional boundaries. Regardless of the debates surrounding them, their influence on the course of globalization is undeniable, making them an essential part of our journey in understanding our connected world.

Chapter 7:
Globalization in the 21st Century

As we journey forward into the 21st century, globalization takes on new dimensions, mirroring the novel challenges and opportunities that our world presents. This chapter unveils the facets of globalization in our current century, casting a light on the significant role that digital advancements play in bringing people closer than ever before. It examines how pandemics, a stark reminder of our interconnectedness, influence globalization processes. Finally, it explores the close relationship between globalization and climate change, a pressing issue that requires a concerted global response. So, buckle up, and prepare for a deep dive into the realities of globalization in the 21st century.

Digital Globalization

The internet - a wondrous space where ideas proliferate, businesses flourish, and connections foster. It is here, in this nebulous world, that digital globalization finds its home. And yet, what is digital globalization? Is it merely the international sharing of cat videos, or is there something more profound at play? Fear not, for we shall unwrap this enigma together, examining its intricacies, and its monumental implications for our world.

In its simplest form, digital globalization refers to the interconnectedness brought about by digital technologies and online platforms. Much like the sailors of old charting new trade routes, we've found ourselves a new frontier. However, instead of traversing the oceans blue, we traverse the world wide web, where data flows freely and borders blur. This novel sphere of globalization has revolutionized communication, making geographical barriers a thing of the past. Information, ideas, and innovation are shared instantaneously across continents.

But it isn't just social media and instant messaging reshaping our world. Let's turn our attention to e-commerce, the bustling marketplaces of the internet. Businesses, both mammoth corporations and local mom-and-pop shops, have an international audience at their fingertips. The democratizing effect of e-commerce allows for a fairer playing field where innovation and quality can shine above sheer size and marketing budget.

Yet, digital globalization doesn't just stop at e-commerce. The digitization of services has made a myriad of resources accessible to anyone with an internet connection. Education has been revolutionized by Massive Open Online Courses (MOOCs), democratizing access to knowledge. Telemedicine brings healthcare to remote communities. Digital banking and cryptocurrencies offer financial services beyond the reach of traditional banking infrastructures.

The impacts of digital globalization are vast and variegated. It's not just the economy that's affected; the cultural landscape is also undergoing seismic shifts. Cultural exchanges are no longer confined to physical travel; they occur at the speed of a click, encouraging a fusion of ideas and promoting mutual understanding among diverse cultures.

However, the sunny shores of digital globalization also host some jagged rocks. The digital divide looms large, threatening to leave behind those without access to the necessary technology or skills. Cybersecurity concerns cast a shadow over our online interactions. The prevalence of disinformation on online platforms can cause confusion and division.

As we progress further into the 21st century, it's evident that digital globalization will continue to shape our societies, economies, and cultures in ways we are only beginning to understand. Like a double-edged sword, it presents both immense opportunities and substantial challenges. Yet, one thing remains clear - digital globalization is here to stay, and navigating its nuances will be essential for our collective future.

So there you have it, an enlightening jaunt through the realms of digital globalization, from the bustling e-marketplaces to the broad plains of cultural exchange. Just remember to hold on to your Wi-Fi signal, for who knows what turn we'll take next on this fascinating journey.

Globalization and Pandemics

In the intricate tapestry of globalization, there are strands that capture the vibrancy of shared cultures, the dynamism of global trade, and the promise of technological progress. But interwoven amongst these, there are also threads of a darker hue – these represent the inherent challenges of an increasingly interconnected world. Among these, one stands starkly prominent: the facilitation of pandemics. As we embark on this exploration, let's keep in mind that even the most somber of colors are essential to the full picture.

In the realm of public health, globalization has always been a double-edged sword. On one hand, it brings about improvements in healthcare delivery, with medical innovations and knowledge sharing across borders. However, on the flip side, it provides a superhighway for infectious diseases to traverse the globe at unprecedented speed. The faster and more frequently we travel, the quicker these viruses can leapfrog from one locale to another.

Take, for example, the jet age. A bug picked up in a Beijing bazaar in the morning could be circulating in a New York subway by evening. With international travel becoming more accessible, pandemics can spread rapidly, leading to a global health crisis within weeks or even days. This narrative has been evident in several global health emergencies in recent history, including SARS, MERS, Ebola, and the profound COVID-19 pandemic.

Global supply chains also play a role in the dynamics of pandemics. As businesses across the world source materials and labor from various corners of the globe, disease transmission is no longer limited to humans. Pathogens can now travel the globe ensconced in agricultural products, wild and domestic animals, and even inanimate objects. This connectedness, while fueling economic growth, has made containment of disease outbreaks incredibly challenging.

In the midst of a pandemic, globalization shines a harsh light on global disparities. Unequal access to healthcare, differences in infrastructure, and disparities in health literacy can lead to starkly contrasting outcomes between countries and within societies. The burden often falls disproportionately on the poor and vulnerable, widening existing social and economic inequalities.

Yet, it's not all doom and gloom. Globalization, while facilitating the spread of pandemics, also provides the tools to combat them. International cooperation in the face of pandemics has led to remarkable feats, from shared research and vaccination development to coordinated containment efforts. The World Health Organization plays a critical role in this context, coordinating global health responses and fostering collaboration.

As we stand in the shadow of a pandemic, it's clear that globalization, with its myriad interconnected threads, is an integral part of the narrative. It reminds us that, in our global village, public health isn't confined by borders. A disease that affects one affects all. Hence, our response, too, should be collective and collaborative.

In the grand story of globalization, pandemics serve as potent reminders of our shared vulnerability and shared responsibility. We're all passengers on this global ship, and an illness in steerage can rapidly reach the captain's deck. As we navigate these troubled waters, it is essential to remember that our fates are interconnected, and the solutions must be too. The winds of globalization may facilitate the spread of pandemics, but they can also carry the seeds of resilience, cooperation, and hope.

Globalization and Climate Change

In this symphony we call globalization, climate change is a discordant note that's becoming increasingly difficult to ignore. It's like that unnoticed crack in a grand old dam that suddenly becomes glaringly evident when the water starts seeping through. And boy, is it seeping through. Globalization, the melody we've been humming along to for decades, is inextricably intertwined with the rhythms of climate change. Let's unpack this concept and its implications with a dash of verve and, dare we say, a touch of swagger.

The intertwining of globalization and climate change is a medley of economic, technological, and political harmonies. Start with economics: global trade means more goods are transported across oceans, skies, and roads, resulting in increasing carbon emissions. Industrialization, a tune familiar to both developed and developing countries, adds its own verses to the song, spewing greenhouse gases into the atmosphere. Here's the crescendo: a voracious appetite for consumer goods, a signature tune of our globalized world, leads to increased production and, consequently, more emissions.

And let's not forget the technology. On one hand, it's playing a wonderful tune: green energy solutions, advances in climate science, and digital platforms to foster international cooperation on climate issues. On the other hand, we have technological advances facilitating resource extraction, energy-intensive cryptocurrency mining, and e-waste generation, which put a strain on our environment and exacerbate climate change.

Politically, globalization gives rise to an ironic situation. The countries contributing the most to climate change through their industrial activities and high-consumption lifestyles are often not the ones facing the music. Low-lying island nations, equatorial countries, and arid regions suffer the most from increased floods, stronger hurricanes, heatwaves, and droughts, even though their contributions to the problem are negligible in comparison.

Yet, in this dissonant composition, there are also harmonious chords. Globalization allows for a global response to a global problem. It offers platforms for international cooperation and facilitates the sharing of best practices and technological solutions. Global movements to fight climate change, such as the Paris Agreement and the

Green New Deal, are possible because of our interconnected world.

Climate change, however, adds a degree of urgency to the score. The current pace of environmental degradation calls for a rapid response, one that outpaces the slow tempo of international diplomacy. It demands a new kind of global symphony, where every nation is an active participant, every citizen a willing orchestra member, and every decision a conscious note in the song of preservation.

In essence, globalization and climate change are conducting a complicated dance, stepping on each other's toes at times, and at others, moving in perfect synchrony. They reflect our globalized world's inherent contradictions: the potential for both creation and destruction, unity and division, harmony and discord.

To end on a positive note, let's remember that the music isn't over yet. We are the composers of this global symphony, and we have the power to introduce a more harmonious melody. After all, globalization doesn't just represent the challenges we face—it embodies the potential solutions too. Through concerted global efforts, we can ensure the song of globalization is one of sustainable development, resilience, and harmony with nature.

Chapter 8:
Critiques of Globalization

In this chapter, we wade into the swirling vortex of controversy surrounding globalization. Some see it as a glimmering highway leading humanity to a prosperous and connected future, while others see it as a runaway train, hurling us towards economic inequity, cultural homogenization, and environmental devastation. But fear not, we are not here to draw a line in the sand, but to illuminate the spectrum of critiques with the torch of understanding. We will delve into economic, social and cultural, and environmental criticisms, exposing the underside of the globalization coin, not to tarnish its shine, but to fully appreciate its complexities. So hold onto your hats, dear explorers, as we navigate the rocky terrain of the critiques of globalization.

Economic Critiques

Economic criticisms of globalization can feel as varied and nuanced as the global market itself. Yet, there are some recurring themes that make regular appearances in these critiques, threading together a tapestry of shared concerns. These shared apprehensions typically orbit around inequality, instability, and the potential for exploitation.

In the realm of inequality, critics point out that while globalization has fostered unprecedented wealth, it has not been evenly distributed. The argument runs that richer nations and multinational corporations reap the lion's share of benefits, while poorer nations struggle to catch up. Critics say that the global market system, driven by profit, favors those with economic power and resources, creating a wealth gap both between and within countries. The plight of the disappearing middle class in developed nations and the minimal movement from poverty in many developing nations are often cited as examples.

Instability is another argument critics of globalization often return to. They argue that the interconnectedness of the global economy means that crises are now more likely to ripple across borders. The 2008 financial crisis, which started in the United States and quickly spread to the rest of the world, is often presented as an example of this type of systemic vulnerability.

Lastly, the issue of exploitation is a bone of contention. Detractors argue that globalization creates a race to the bottom in terms of labor and environmental standards. Countries eager for investment may downplay these standards, leading to poor working conditions and environmental degradation. The relentless pursuit of the lowest production costs can drive companies to exploit workers in countries with lax labor laws and lower wages, sometimes resulting in what critics label as 'modern-day slavery.'

Of course, these critiques are not universally accepted. Proponents of globalization often present counterarguments, highlighting the overall increase in living standards, the potential for economic recovery, and market-based solutions to exploitation. Yet, these economic criticisms persist, forcing economists and policy-makers to grapple with the question: How can we make globalization work for everyone?

Social and Cultural Critiques

While the economic criticisms of globalization are plentiful, they are but one facet of a larger critique. Social and cultural criticisms abound, often focusing on the impact globalization has on community cohesion, cultural diversity, and human rights.

On the community level, critics point to the potential corrosive effects of globalization. They argue that the pursuit of global market integration can lead to a sense of dislocation and loss of local identity. In other words, as businesses, economies, and governments become more interconnected, individuals may feel more alienated and powerless. This sense of dislocation can manifest in various forms, from mental health issues to a growing sense of xenophobia and nationalism.

Cultural critics express concerns about the homogenizing effects of globalization. They fear that the global spread of Western, and more specifically American, culture might lead to a sort of cultural imperialism. This can result in a loss of cultural diversity as smaller cultures struggle to survive against the onslaught of dominant ones. Moreover, the critics argue, this cultural homogenization can lead to a sense of cultural dislocation and alienation, particularly among indigenous populations and minority groups.

Finally, human rights concerns are often raised within the context of social and cultural criticisms. Critics point out that while globalization can spread ideas of human rights, it can also exacerbate human rights abuses. For instance, in the race to offer the cheapest labor or the most attractive tax conditions, some countries may overlook or outright ignore issues such as child labor, exploitation of workers, or suppression of political dissent.

Just as with economic criticisms, these social and cultural critiques are met with counterarguments. Proponents of globalization argue that it can foster intercultural understanding, spread liberal values, and lead to social improvements through economic development. Nonetheless, the persistence of these criticisms demonstrates that globalization is a complex, multifaceted phenomenon whose impacts are deeply felt on both societal and personal levels.

Environmental Critiques

The environmental critiques of globalization form a crucial part of the larger critique, especially in a time when our planet faces significant environmental challenges. These concerns typically focus on the role of globalization in aggravating climate change, promoting unsustainable consumption, and leading to loss of biodiversity.

Climate change has become one of the most pressing issues of our time, and globalization is frequently implicated in its acceleration. Global economic integration often leads to increased production, consumption, and consequently, greenhouse gas emissions. The massive expansion of global trade has resulted in a significant rise in transport emissions, particularly from shipping and aviation.

The critique extends to the patterns of consumption promoted by globalization. Critics argue that a global culture of consumerism, driven by multinational corporations, encourages unsustainable levels of resource use. This consumerist culture often glorifies disposable products, leading to an increase in waste generation and contributing to the global waste management crisis. Moreover, the pursuit of natural resources to fuel global growth can lead to the exploitation of countries rich in these resources, often with little regard for local environments or communities.

The loss of biodiversity is another significant environmental critique. The expansion of global markets can lead to habitat destruction as forests are cut down to make way for agricultural land or mined for resources. The spread of monocultures in agriculture, driven by the global food market, can also result in loss of local plant varieties, negatively impacting biodiversity. Moreover, globalization can contribute to the spread of invasive species that harm local ecosystems.

Yet, it's also worth noting that globalization, with its capacity for rapid dissemination of information and ideas, offers opportunities to address these environmental challenges. For instance, international agreements on climate change and biodiversity are only possible because of our interconnected world. Nevertheless, the severity of these environmental critiques underlines the urgency of making our global system more sustainable, and ensuring that the forces of globalization are harnessed to protect, rather than harm, our planet.

Chapter 9:
The Future of Globalization

As we step into the final part of our exploration of globalization, we'll gaze into the potential future that awaits us in an increasingly connected world. This section will sketch out possible scenarios for globalization's evolution, diving into the key factors that could shape this trajectory. We'll also examine the likely impact on our work and lifestyle as a consequence of these global shifts. From technological breakthroughs to environmental challenges, political decisions to cultural evolution, this winding road to the future is ripe with complexities and uncertainties. Let's unravel this mystery together and perhaps, shed some light on the path that lies ahead.

Potential Scenarios

Peering into the future of globalization, we see a tableau of diverse potential scenarios unfolding in front of us. Our journey begins with a continuation of current trends, where increased interconnectivity fosters a more intertwined global community. Trade and technology might continue their waltz hand-in-hand, reaching an unprecedented level of economic integration. The transformation might be so profound that the national borders fade in economic terms.

However, an alternate scenario could be a backlash against globalization, influenced by a combination of nationalistic sentiments, economic inequalities, and security concerns. In such a scenario, we might witness countries prioritizing their own economic well-being over international cooperation, leading to a resurgence of protectionist policies.

Globalization might take a more regional character, with trading blocs becoming more critical, while global institutions lose their influence.

The most dramatic twist in our plot could be a global paradigm shift triggered by an unforeseen event— much like how the Covid-19 pandemic upended the world. Such large-scale disruptions could necessitate a complete rethink of our economic systems, possibly paving the way for a form of globalization that is radically different from what we understand today.

As our technologies advance, we could see the emergence of a digital-first globalization, or "Globalization 4.0" if you will. This scenario paints a picture of a world where digital connections and virtual collaboration are the prime drivers of global integration, reducing the physical distances even more dramatically.

Finally, we must consider an environmentally-centered scenario. Here, our response to the climate crisis shapes the trajectory of globalization. It could be a world that sees an unprecedented level of global cooperation to combat climate change, or conversely, one where resource scarcity triggers competition and conflict, dampening the spirits of globalization.

The future, as they say, is a mysterious land. We can chart our maps and plan our journeys, but we must remember that the road ahead can always surprise us. Let's pack our bags and get ready to navigate these possible paths, keeping in mind that the future of globalization is as much about creation as it is about adaptation.

Influencing Factors

The scenery of the future isn't painted on a blank canvas. Instead, it's built on a complex mosaic of elements - the influencing factors. As we peer into the misty horizon of globalization's future, it's worth pondering the key factors that will steer its course.

Technology has been and will continue to be the vanguard of globalization. The continuing evolution of artificial intelligence, robotics, quantum computing, and other advanced technologies will push the boundaries of global connectivity, shaping how we work, communicate, and interact. The phenomenon of digital globalization may transform the very fabric of our global village, blurring the physical boundaries between nations.

Economic dynamics will also play a pivotal role. Changes in global economic power - be it the rise of emerging economies, shifts in trade dynamics, or the evolution of economic systems - will affect the pace and nature of globalization. Factors like foreign direct investment, global financial stability, and the state of global commodity markets will continue to impact the ebbs and flows of global integration.

The global political landscape too will mold the contours of globalization. A world order where multilateralism is strengthened could usher in a phase of accelerated globalization. Conversely, an ascendant trend of nationalism or regionalism could prompt countries to erect walls, slowing down the integration process.

Environmental considerations are no longer a footnote in any discourse, and it's no different here. The unfolding climate crisis, the quest for sustainability, and our responses to these challenges will shape globalization's trajectory. Will the fight against climate change necessitate unprecedented global cooperation, or could resource scarcity trigger conflict and disrupt globalization?

Then, there are the sociocultural factors. Trends like the global spread of English, the impact of social media on culture and values, the global social justice movements, and the blending and clashing of cultures will influence the shape of our global society.

Lastly, the unexpected must always have a seat at the table when we talk about the future. Large-scale disruptions, be they pandemics, natural disasters, or groundbreaking innovations, can have seismic impacts on the path of globalization.

As we walk this tightrope towards the future, it's important to remember that these factors aren't isolated elements but intricately connected threads of the same tapestry. It's the dynamic interplay between them that will write the next chapter of our global narrative. Buckle up, it's going to be quite the ride.

Globalization and the Future of Work

The map of the global workplace is perpetually being redrawn, and globalization plays a leading role in drafting its contours. In the chapters ahead, we'll delve into the fascinating interplay between globalization and the future of work, and how it's set to redefine our professional lives.

The rise of remote work and virtual teams, hastened by the digital revolution and recent pandemic experiences, is making the global village a workplace reality. Geographic boundaries are vanishing as companies harness global talent pools, and workers from different time zones collaborate in real-time. In the future, your colleague could be as likely to be living halfway across the globe as next door.

Globalization is also pushing the envelope on the gig economy. The expanding online marketplace for freelancers is transforming the way we think about jobs and employment. No longer are jobs tied to a physical location, a nine-to-five schedule, or even a long-term contract. This shift towards more flexible work arrangements is likely to continue, transforming traditional labor markets.

Then there's the fascinating but slightly unnerving dance between automation, artificial intelligence, and work. While the automatons aren't on the brink of an employment coup just yet, technology is certainly reshaping job profiles and skills demands. Jobs of the future may require a new breed of digital literacy, innovative thinking, and the ability to work alongside AI.

Globalization is also bringing diverse voices and perspectives into the workplace. Companies are becoming more multicultural, multi-generational, and inclusive. As we move towards a future of work that celebrates diversity, businesses will need to develop inclusive work policies that embrace these differences, leading to a richer, more creative, and more productive work environment.

Education and training systems will also need to keep up with the rapid pace of change in the globalized work environment. Skills training will have to be lifelong, dynamic, and adaptable, preparing workers for an evolving labor market and encouraging continual learning and growth.

There are, of course, challenges on this journey. Issues like fair wages, workers' rights, and ensuring equal opportunities in an increasingly digital and global job market remain paramount. Addressing these issues in a globalized context will require international cooperation and effective governance.

As we peer into the kaleidoscope of the future, it's clear that globalization will continue to be a game-changer in the arena of work. Strap in, because the future of work is likely to be as dynamic and diverse as our interconnected world itself.

Conclusion

In our concluding chapter, we draw together the many threads of our global tapestry, illuminating the complex yet enthralling picture that is globalization. We'll distill lessons learned from our journey and reflect upon the significant role globalization plays in our daily lives and the future of our shared world. From historical contexts, driving forces, impacts, critiques, and prospective scenarios, to the intricate dance with the future of work, this will be an opportunity to reflect, learn, and consider the path ahead in this globalized age.

Lessons Learned

The symphony of globalization has many parts and each part plays a role in the composition of the whole. We've journeyed through the historical precedents of globalization, examined the forces that drive it, and analyzed its impacts on different regions and populations. In this section, we pause to contemplate and understand the key lessons we have learned from our exploration.

Lesson one is the immense resilience and adaptability of human societies. Across epochs, human societies have faced numerous challenges and opportunities brought about by globalization. Each time, communities have evolved, adapted, and harnessed the forces at play, showcasing a robust resilience that is profoundly inspiring.

Lesson two, globalization is not an isolated phenomenon but rather is deeply intertwined with technological advancements, economic progress, social shifts, and political landscapes. Recognizing these interconnections allows us to understand the multifaceted nature of globalization and to predict and respond to its future implications more effectively.

The third lesson is the understanding that globalization is not a zero-sum game. It's a complex puzzle where benefits and drawbacks coexist. For some, globalization has opened doors to unprecedented opportunities, while for others, it has presented formidable challenges. Balancing these contrasting outcomes remains an ongoing global endeavor.

The fourth lesson to note is the critical role of institutions in managing globalization. From the United Nations to the World Trade Organization, these bodies have demonstrated that global cooperation and shared governance are crucial for managing the complexities of a globalized world.

Finally, the fifth lesson learned is the profound influence of globalization on our future work landscape. As technological advances reshape the work world, we are called to continuously adapt, learn, and innovate. Embracing lifelong learning is more important than ever in this globalized era.

These lessons offer us crucial insights, illuminating the path forward as we continue to navigate the enthralling saga of globalization. By learning from the past and present, we can shape a future that harnesses the potential of globalization while mitigating its challenges.

Final Reflections

As we wrap up our exploration of "Our Connected World", it's fitting to pause for a final reflection, stepping back to look at the larger picture that we've painted together. We began our journey in the far-reaching past, threading our way through the narrative of globalization, exploring its impacts, the forces that propel it, the institutions that guide it, and glimpsing the myriad ways it shapes our lives.

From the interwoven tapestry of cultures to the pulsating arteries of international trade, from the ceaseless waves of technological innovation to the pressing global challenges we face, globalization is as intricate as it is omnipresent. It is the invisible hand that has, over the ages, gently nudged humanity closer together, while sometimes pushing us apart.

Yet, as we've discovered, it isn't an invincible force. Instead, globalization is a living, breathing process, shaped as much by us as we are by it. It mirrors our collective aspirations, our shared struggles, and our enduring capacity for change. It's a narrative that evolves with each passing moment, every human interaction, every technological breakthrough, every policy decision.

As we glance ahead, we are confronted with a future that is uncertain yet rife with possibilities. Will the next chapter of globalization bring us closer together or widen the gulf between us? Will it usher in an age of shared prosperity or deepen the scars of inequality? As we stand on the brink of tomorrow, these questions loom large, reminding us of our shared responsibility.

But let us not forget, we are not passive spectators in this unfolding drama. Each one of us, in our own unique way, contributes to the story of globalization. By engaging with the world around us, by making informed decisions, by advocating for inclusive and sustainable practices, we can actively influence the trajectory of globalization.

In this grand narrative, we are both the storytellers and the protagonists. The chapters ahead are blank pages, waiting for us to fill them. As we pen our stories, let us draw on the lessons of the past, the realities of the present, and the promise of a shared future. Let us remember that our actions, no matter how small, ripple outwards, shaping the contours of our connected world.

In the end, perhaps, that is the greatest revelation of our journey through "Our Connected World": that we are, indeed, interconnected in myriad ways. And it is through these connections, these shared threads of humanity, that we can create a global story that resonates with hope, understanding, and shared prosperity.

About the Author

Thomas T. Taylor is a man of many titles. In his hometown, he's known as "Mr. Friendly," a testament to his warm demeanor and unwavering dedication to his community. In the realm of academia, he's a scholar with a rich background in social psychology and political science. In the political sphere, he's a seasoned veteran, having immersed himself in local politics since his early twenties.

Taylor's journey into politics was not a career choice, but a calling. His early involvement in the political scene has given him an intimate understanding of the inner workings of governance and the pivotal role of community engagement. His approachability and commitment to his constituents have not only earned him the nickname "Mr. Friendly" but also the respect and trust of his community.

Complementing his political endeavors, Taylor's academic pursuits in social psychology and political science have provided him with a profound understanding of the societal dynamics that underpin politics. He seamlessly bridges the gap between theoretical knowledge and practical application, leveraging his academic insights to foster a more inclusive and balanced political environment.

Away from the public eye, Taylor leads a fulfilling family life. He is a loving husband and a doting father to six children. His family serves as a constant reminder of the real-world impact of political decisions, reinforcing the importance of building a society that values fairness, compassion, and understanding.

In his book, "Rebuilding Democracy: Strategies for Countering Political Extremism", Taylor brings together his wealth of political experience, academic expertise, and personal reflections. He offers a comprehensive guide to understanding and countering political extremism, hoping to inspire readers to renew their commitment to democratic values and to actively contribute to a more inclusive and balanced political discourse.

www.ingramcontent.com/pod-product-compliance
Lightning Source LLC
Chambersburg PA
CBHW031400060726

47590CB00007B/2873